The Definition Of A Man

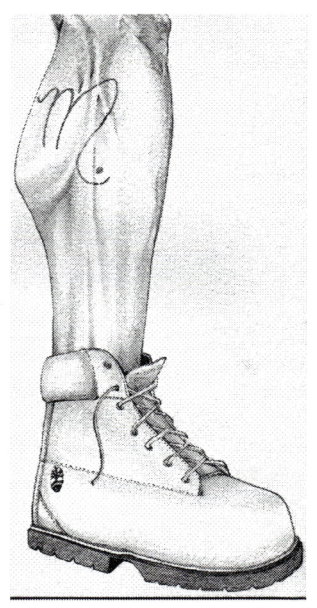

by Marcel Byes

Marcel Byes

Unless otherwise indicated, all scripture quotations are taken from *The Original King James Version of the Bible. Copyright* © *1977*

"The Definition Of A Man"
ISBN 1-59872-709-5
Copyright © 2006 by Marcel Byes
Los Angeles, CA 90044
All rights reserved under the seal of Copyright Office in accordance with title 17 United States Code, registration number TXu1-317-807.

Art design on cover by Kevin Howard.

The Definition

Of

A Man

by Marcel Byes

Marcel Byes

About the Author

Marcel Byes, born and raised in Erie, Pennsylvania, graduated from a Technical High School where he majored in Machine Shop. Later, he furthered his education at Erie Vocational College, taking classes in Machine Math and Tool & Die. After graduating, Marcel worked in the Tool & Die Industry for more than twelve years.

While working as a Machinist, Marcel received a calling on his life to mentor young Men. Taking heed to his calling, he started taking Bible classes at

Marcel Byes

a Christian Center in Erie, Pennsylvania. At the same time, he enrolled in a leadership class held at the center, as well. The teachers and leaders at the center noticed something special in Marcel, and suggested he study more and prepare himself for a rigorous course in becoming an Elder of the center. Being obedient, Marcel took the course and was ordained an Elder in 1996.

After accepting the call as an Elder, Marcel taught classes on Manhood and leadership, with most of his students being young Men. Eventually, his dedication and commitment afforded him the opportunity to teach the entire congregation. While teaching, he still worked as a Machinist, and just by his lifestyle, he caught the attention of a fellow Machinist who eventually asked Marcel to speak at a Men's conference held in Girard, Pennsylvania. it was his largest speaking engagement, and many of the Men were inspired by the powerful message. Since then, Marcel has mentored many young Men in various cities, such as Atlanta, GA; Raleigh, NC; and Los Angeles, CA.

He currently resides in Los Angeles, California, and has one son and two daughters.

Marcel Byes

The Definition Of A Man

Acknowledgements

To my son, Lavar, who is the inspiration that led me to seek what real Manhood is, so I might show you by example how to be a real Man.

To my beautiful daughters, Brittany and Bradaja: I pray I will be the same example of a Man you will notice when it's time for you to choose. Daddy loves you!

And last, to my friend Carla M. Dean, thank you for your great editing work.

Marcel Byes

Dedication

This book is dedicated to my mother, Ruby Gillespie. Thanks, mom, for all your love and support. You raised a good one, and now I get to share a little of your love with the world.

I love you.

Marcel Byes

The Definition Of A Man

Contents

Introduction
~Page 15

Chapter One:
A Real Man Knows His Purpose In Life
~Page 17

Chapter Two:
A Real Man Has Only One Woman/Wife
~Page 25

Chapter Three:
A Real Man Controls Lust
~Page 29

Chapter Four:
A Real Man Puts God First
~Page 35

Chapter Five:
A Real Man Doesn't Lie
~Page 41

Chapter Six:
A Real Man Accepts A Woman's Nature
~Page 45

Closing
~Page 51

Marcel Byes

The Definition Of A Man

Introduction

We all know a Man should have integrity, be the provider for his family, and play the part of a role model to his children. However, responsibility goes much deeper than that!

Come with me on this journey into the "Definition Of A Man." I do not profess to be a Pastor or a Bible scholar, but through study and experience, I share my opinion on what *real* Manhood is.

In the dictionary, the definition of a Man is "An Adult Male." My goal with this book is to prove there is so much more to manhood than just being "An Adult Male."

Marcel Byes

Chapter One

A Real Man Knows His Purpose In Life

The quickest and best definition I could give you of a Man would be, whatever God says a Man is. Then, we could close the book right now, because it is true. A Man *is* whatever God says a Man is. He is the one who created us in His own image, so who would know better than The Creator?

The first Man that God created was Adam, and he was the epitome of what God says a Man should be (Genesis 2:7). He (Adam) had dominion over everything God created, ie: land, sea, animals, etc. (Genesis 1:26). So, Adam had a purpose for existing. even though he blew it, he still had a purpose for existing.

The Definition Of A Man

We all have our own specific purpose for living. But how do we find out what our purpose is? I am glad you asked! I was once taught the way to find your purpose is by figuring out what upsets or angers you the most in life, and then find a solution for that particular problem. However, I believe in the power of prayer, and I believe God answers prayer by depositing thoughts or sending someone to deliver an answer to your prayer. So, if you do not know your purpose in life, pray and ask God what that purpose is.

I found out my purpose while staying at a homeless shelter. No, I was not homeless. However, one morning, my wife (who is now my ex-wife) and I had a big argument, and I became so angry I had to leave the house. So, I left and started walking. I swear I could have walked for days. That's how much steam I needed to let off. Eventually, I ended up at the Greyhound bus station, and just sat there

Marcel Byes

for hours with smoke coming from my ears, not wanting to talk to anybody.

I knew my family would be worried with me being gone for so long, but I refused to return home. I didn't know what to do. I was confused, a nervous wreck. So, I went to the front desk at the bus station and asked how much a ticket to Akron, Ohio would cost. At the time, I was living in Erie, Pennsylvania. I hadn't been many places outside of Erie, but I used to go to Akron to watch an old high school friend of mine play football. After the clerk told me the price would be forty dollars, I purchased the ticket and was on the next bus to Akron, Ohio, with no specific destination in mind when I arrived there.

Half the day had passed, and I still hadn't called home. I knew by this point my family was worried sick.

The Definition Of A Man

I arrived at the bus station in Akron still confused and angry. It had been years since I talked to my old football buddy, and I had no idea if he still lived in Akron. So, I decided to look through the phone book to see if I could find a listing for him, and I did. In fact, I found a lot of listings with the same name as his! Faced with no other choice, I began calling the numbers one by one, but had no success locating the number belonging to my buddy. Finally, I gave up. There I sat at the bus station in Akron, Ohio, not knowing anyone there, with only about sixty dollars in my pocket, and without a coat on my back. What in the heck was I thinking?

I'm sure you're asking what does this story has to do with Manhood? Trust me, I'll get there.

I left the bus station, walking but not knowing where the heck I was going. I thought about getting a cheap motel room, but then remembered I had to get myself back to Erie and would need the money I had left to do so. While walking a busy street in downtown Akron, I noticed a homeless shelter and entered. Looking around, I saw it was full of Men, young and old. The guy at the front desk asked if he could help me, and I told him I needed a place to stay.

His first response was "you're joking, right? You dont look like a guy that should be here." In the back of my mind, I was thinking, *you're right. I shouldn't be here!* Instead, I told him I really needed a place to stay. Without any further delay, he checked my I.D. and welcomed me.

So, there I was, twenty-seven years old, sitting in a homeless shelter while my wife and kids were at home worrying about me. I later found out my wife had called everyone looking for me, including filing a missing person's report with the police station. still, I refused to call home.

As I sat in that homeless shelter, I witnessed Men coming in left and right. Some of them knew the

The Definition Of A Man

guy at the front desk by name, signifying to me they'd been there many times before, which they had. It was getting late and time for bed, but of course, I couldn't sleep because I felt so out of place. I began to pray and ask God what I was doing there. At that moment, God spoke to me and told me that my purpose in life was to be a mentor and show young Men this kind of living is unacceptable and how God has so much more planned for them. These Men had made this place their home, and God let me know he wanted me to help young Men take their rightful place in life and be an example by living a lifestyle one could imitate. He (God) also told me to get my butt back home to my wife and kids!

I shared that story with you to show that sometimes in order to hear from God you have to get away from everything…maybe not to my extreme, but away from the norm. Then you will know it is God speaking to you. and then, you can ask God… what

Marcel Byes

am I doing here? *A Real Man Knows His Purpose In Life!*

Needless to say, I was on the first bus back to Erie the next morning!

Chapter Two
A Real Man Has Only One Woman/Wife

For many years, Men have tried to justify cheating on their women by comparing themselves to Men in the Bible that had multiple wives and concubines (girlfriends). However, please notice God's first Man (Adam) had but only one woman, Eve. I believe if cheating was intended to be a part of our nature, or if God felt we needed more than one woman, he (God) would have given Adam more than just one woman.

As Men, God has given us such a strong nature that we are able to refrain from any obstacle that comes our way and the only one who renders that power is ourselves, whether it's good or bad. Unfortunately, after Adam chose to render his nature for the bad, with the great sin of disobedience (Genesis 3:6), that is when we started reading of men with multiple wives and concubines. God has always intended for Man to have but one woman. However, if we render that strong God-given nature, we will choose to have more. Notice I said *choose*. We indeed have a choice, so make the right one!

I believe we need to view Adam as he was before his great sin, and that should be our role model. Again, God created Adam to be the epitome of what a *Real Man* should be, which includes having one woman!

Now, I know many of you are probably saying Adam is the reason we are in the mess we're in today, which is true. However, before Adam sinned, he was The Definition Of A Man. That is why the Bible tells us we are co-workers with God (1 Corinthians 3:9). He wants us to help bring back *real* Manhood.

The Definition Of A Man

We may not be able to go back to the Garden of Eden, but while we're here on this earth, one woman is enough for a *Real* Man. Anything contrary is not Manhood!

Marcel Byes

Chapter Three
A Real Man Controls Lust

I believe in spiritual warfare. I believe there are Angels and Demons in constant battle over our bodies every day, hour, minute, and second. The Demon's job is to destroy us, while the Angel's job is to spare us to abundant living. If you ever get a chance, please read *This Present Darkness* by Frank E. Peretti and you'll see exactly what I'm talking about.

Thoughts are deposited in our heads constantly, and it's up to us to control them. When we do, we give the Angels the upperhand in the battle. Let me explain what I'm talking about...

Marcel Byes

I use to love watching music videos with skimpy dressed, voluptuous women dancing around. I mean, I would be glued to the television with all sorts of thoughts running through my head on what I would do to the women. I would lock her image in my mind, and later, when alone, I would regenerate that image and imagine I was having sex with her. I had it bad!

It was the "M" word, also known as masturbation. my thoughts were loaded with unpure images, and masturbation had become a regular thing for me. I knew I wasn't being *real* and it became a problem. I was hooked. I knew this couldn't be of God, because I was lusting after these images and I know lust is not of God.

The Bible tells us to cast down every imagination and bring it in to captivity according to the Word Of God (2 Corinthians 10:5), which means we must capture every single thought and decide what we're going to do with it. The Bible also gives us measuring devices to determine if a thought needs to be thrown out or kept. (Remember, we have Angels and Demons that deposit thoughts.) Those measuring devices are things that are True, Honest, Righteous, Pure, Lovely, and a Good Report (Philippians 4:8). Therefore, if that thought is not all of these things, it must be discarded! and you're the one who has to throw it out.

Look carefully at what I said..."if it's not *All* of these things." some bad thoughts might have one or more of those traits, but it must be *all* of these: True, Honest, Righteous, Pure, Lovely, and a Good Report. If it's not, then throw it out! I know that's easier said than done, but until we get to that point, we'll never experience *Real* Manhood.

I did not stop masturbating cold turkey, although it is possible. It was a process. First, I had to ask God to deliver me. Next, I had to stop watching those videos and get my thoughts in line. Then, it was a wrap! remember, A *Real* Man Controls His Lust!

Marcel Byes

The Definition Of A Man

Chapter Four
A Real Man Puts God First

No, I'm not talking about going to church every Sunday, or joining the deacon board, the usher board, the Men's board, or all those other boards. I'm talking about putting God first in everything you do.

There is a very familiar scripture in the Bible that says, "Seek Ye First The Kingdom Of God And His Rightousness And All These Things Will Be Added To You" (Matthew 6:33).

I was heavily involved at a former church I use to attend. I was on the Men's board, taught Sunday

The Definition Of A Man

School and youth classes, and took classes on leadership. It was where I first tapped into what *Real* Manhood is.

In 1996, I was ordained an Elder of the church. I wanted to live right, be a *Real* Man of God, so I got married, brought a few friends to Christ, studied the Bible regularly, etc. Some things started happening at church that I did not agree with, so I resigned from that church. One day, I made up my mind that I wanted to be a star. That's when I started pursuing stardom. Soon, I was having problems in my marriage, which ended in a divorce. By now, I had been detered from church and the things of God.

My first step to stardom, or so I thought, was to start my own clothing line. I designed a clothing line called "Mooch Gear," the buzz got around locally, and stores started selling my clothes. My hometown was really supportive and embraced the clothing line, so I kinda became a local star. But I wanted more. So, I traveled to different cities to promote my clohing line on a larger scale. Everything was going really good. I started selling clothes, having fashion shows, etc. now "Mooch Gear' was making a name for itself. The money was good, and at the same time, I met many celebrities. I thought I was the Man! but where was God? I put Him on hold!

After just brief success, I had to put "Mooch Gear" on hold and start working a regular job again since my money had run short. Still, I was determined to be a star. I started taking acting classes, moved to Los Angeles, and got an agent so I could be the next best thing, but it didn't happen. I was just spinning my wheels, but going nowhere. That is, until I realized I had my priorities out of wack.

I was putting everything before God. In fact, I was ignoring God and nothing was going my way. Yeah, I met a few celebrities and made great new friends, but my journey was feeling lifeless until I put God back on top. Once I did that, things started going in

The Definition Of A Man

my favor, and if you're reading this book, I even reached that stardom I was seeking so desperately, along with carrying out my purpose to mentor.

The scripture in the Bible that says "Seek Ye First The Kingdom Of God..." is telling us to seek God's rules and regulations on life and everything else will fall into place.

I shared my journey with you to show how you can be chasing a dream and seem to be doing so well, but *Real* Manhood won't manifest until you put God first!

Marcel Byes

Chapter Five
A Real Man Doesn't Lie

No, I'm not just talking about the big lies, like lying to your wife or your girlfriend. I'm talking about lying period! All lies! Those lies that have followed us for most of our lives; Those lies we use to get ahead in life, like claiming kids on your income tax return that are not yours or you haven't cared for, or lying on your resume to impress employers. Those little white lies you use as excuses for missing work, or even the so-called "harmless" lies, like telling bill collectors you're not home. Yeah, those lies!

All lies are harmful to your relationship with God. no matter how big or small, it is still a lie. When you lie, that is saying you have no Faith in God. He (God) can't move on your behalf if your relationship with Him is built on a lie. Just think about it: whatever the reason for your lies, you are only trying to please the person for your benefit. Stop trying to please everyone and Man-up to the situation! God's got your back.

Sometimes we lie because we believe the truth will make us suffer, but the Bible says the truth will make us free (John 8:32). Lying causes us to constantly have to look over our shoulders. Lying causes us to tell more lies to cover up the previous lies. It's an evil and contagious cycle that causes Men to get caught up and move further and further away from God.

There's a scripture in the Bible that says, "Delight Yourself In The Lord And He Will Give You the Desires Of Your Heart" (Psalms 37:4). As Men, we need to delight ourselves in the things of God, but what does that mean? It literally means, if you

The Definition Of A Man

make up your mind to get on God's side of the fence and not be motivated by Money, Power, and Sex, but instead be motivated by Faith and the Love of God, there will be no reason to lie about anything, because then you will know that God has your back!

A Real Man Doesn't Lie

Marcel Byes

Chapter Six

A Real Man Accepts A Woman's Nature

How do we understand a woman's nature? I'm glad you asked! and when you find out, please call me.

When God created Eve from Adam's rib, I don't recall him (God) telling Adam the way she would act. One thing I do remember is God telling him that she would be there so he wouldn't be alone and to be his helpmate (Genesis 2:18).

Again, I'm going back to the first Man and woman God created because that is where our true definition comes from. Of course, after Adam's great sin many prophets came to try and give us an understanding of woman, but I don't believe Man is

Marcel Byes

suppose to understand a woman's nature, but We must accept it! Please understand I'm not saying accept being treated any kind of way, but I'm talking about the God-given nature of a woman.

Many Men have mothers, wives, sisters, and daughters, so I am sure you'll feel me when I'm finished with this chapter.

Now, for the life of me, I'll never figure out how a woman can go to the mall, stop at every store (twice), try on one hundred outfits, two hundred pair of shoes, and come home with only one pair of stockings. I just don't get it! And why when I'm watching my favorite sports program on television is that the same time she wants to talk or be intimate? I know y'all have been there. Please let me try to explain... **There Is No Explanation!**

The Definition Of A Man

God gave Man a certain nature and he gave woman a nature, as well, which are total opposites. It's not our job to figure it out, but we must accept it!

I believe one of the reasons some Men hit women is because they can't figure women out, and so they become frustrated and resort to violence. Please be clear that I said "one" of the reasons. However, the number one reason is because he is not a *Real* Man. if he has to hit a woman, he is not a Man at all! in fact, it's downright shameful! A woman's nature is God given, and what God has given no Man can take away! so, stop trying!

A woman needs security. I know many women have done well on their own for many years and are very independent, but I believe it is in God's divine will that Man provide security to their woman.

What is security? Security is one who gives or assures safety, or to fulfill the obligation of another. God gave Adam dominion over everything (land, sea, animals, etc.), so do you think Eve did not feel secure? This Man (Adam) could have called a lion to his defense if he needed to. So, Men, get in a position to secure your woman and stop trying to figure out why she acts the way she does. Something made you fall in love with her in the beginning, so go back and accept it, because it's in her nature!

I believe a successful relationship between a Man and a woman starts at the very beginning. First, there must be some common grounds established, ie: both are Christians, both share spiritual beliefs, both love children, etc. A lot of Men are blinded by beauty and believe they will be able to convince a woman to see things their way, which is not always the case. Trust God to send that one special woman who has similiar interests as you. God knows what you want, so put your trust in him. Once those things are established and you find common interest, the next step should be honesty. Men, be straight up in the beginning to save headaches down the road. I'm no marraige counselor, but I

The Definition Of A Man

believe that is a good recipe if we're talking about *Real* Manhood.

Real Men Accepts A Woman's Nature!

Marcel Byes

Closing

How long will we continue to mistreat our women? How long will we continue to give our sons false evidence of Manhood? How long will we continue telling lies? How long before we put our pride aside and walk by Faith?

How long before we find "The Definition Of A Man"?

The End

The Definition Of A Man

Other books by Marcel Byes…"From The Mind Of Mooch", Coming 2007

Contact Inforfmation:

marcelbyes@hotmail.com

www.myspace.com/marcelbyes

(919) 395-7536

Marcel Byes

The Definition Of A Man

Marcel Byes